Unleash the Power of Web3: A Beginner's Guide for Non-Techies!

Ralph Kuepper

Copyright © 2023 Ralph Kuepper

All rights reserved.

CONTENTS

Table of Contents

Introduction 1

Introduction to Web3 2

The Problems with the Current Internet 5

Decentralization 8

Privacy in web3 11

Censorship Resistance 14

Trust and Security 17

Economic Empowerment 20

Decentralized Applications 23

The Future of Web3 27

Investment Opportunities 30

Technical Aspects of web3 36

web3 Pitfalls and Risks 39

Conclusion 42

INTRODUCTION
Introduction

Web3 is a decentralized technology reshaping the internet as we know it. It is a new and improved version of the internet that promises to provide users with greater control over their data and online identities, eliminate intermediaries, and promote a more secure and equitable online environment. This collection of chapters will delve into the various aspects of Web3 and underlying technology, including blockchain, cryptography, and consensus algorithms. We will explore the benefits of decentralization, user privacy protection, censorship resistance, trust and security, economic empowerment, and the future of Web3. Additionally, we will examine the potential investment opportunities in Web3 and the exciting new decentralized applications built on this revolutionary platform. Finally, we will address decentralized technology's challenges and potential drawbacks and critically analyze the risks associated with Web3. Whether you are a beginner or an experienced professional, this collection of chapters provides a comprehensive overview of the exciting world of Web3 and its potential for the future of the internet.

How to read this book?

This book is written with standalone chapters that can be read together or separately. Each chapter covers a topic relevant to understanding web3 and is kept concise while discussing all relevant issues.

INTRODUCTION TO WEB3
Introduction to Web3

The internet has revolutionized how we communicate, access information, and do business. However, despite its many benefits, the current internet is facing several challenges that limit its potential and hinder its growth. One of the most pressing problems is centralization, which gives a few large companies control most of the internet's content and data. This centralization has led to several privacy and security issues, censorship, and restriction of access to information.

Web3 represents the next generation of the internet, built on decentralized technology. It puts users in control of their online presence and data. This shift from the centralized architecture of the current internet to a decentralized one is of crucial importance, as it offers solutions to many of the most pressing problems facing the current internet.

In this chapter, we will introduce the basics of decentralized technology and explain how Web3 differs from the current internet. We will also explore the potential impact of Web3 on various aspects of society and the opportunities it presents for a more open, secure, and trustworthy internet.

What is Decentralized Technology?

Decentralized technology refers to a network architecture where data and processing power are distributed across multiple nodes rather than controlled by a central authority. In a decentralized network, each node has an equal role in maintaining and updating the network. As a result, there is no single point of failure.

The most well-known example of decentralized technology is the blockchain. This distributed ledger records transactions securely and transparently. A blockchain network is maintained by a network of nodes, and once a block is added to the chain, it cannot be altered or deleted. This makes blockchains ideal for applications where trust and security are paramount, such as digital currencies and other financial applications.

Decentralized technology also has the potential to be applied in other areas, such as the internet, where it can provide a more secure and trustworthy platform for communication, commerce, and information sharing.

What is Web3?

Web3 refers to the following internet generation, built on decentralized technology. It puts users in control of their online presence and data. Unlike the current internet, which is controlled by a few large companies, Web3 is a decentralized network where users can control their online identity, data, and assets.

Web3 also enables new decentralized applications (dapps) that can run on the network, giving users more control over their online experience. For example, in Web3, users can own and control their data and have the ability to monetize it by selling it to companies that need it.

One of the most significant benefits of Web3 is that it provides a more secure and trustworthy platform for transactions and information sharing. Decentralized technology eliminates the need for intermediaries and reduces the risk of central points of failure, which are often targets for hackers and cybercriminals.

The Impact of Web3

The impact of Web3 is far-reaching and can transform how we interact with the internet and each other. The shift from a centralized to a decentralized architecture will change the power dynamics of the internet, putting users in control of their online presence and data. This can revolutionize how we protect our privacy and personal information and access and share it with others. With the help of decentralized technology and encryption algorithms, Web3 provides a more secure and privacy-friendly platform where users can keep their data safe from third-party companies and cyber criminals.

Additionally, Web3 is designed to be censorship-resistant, providing a platform for free expression and exchanging ideas, even in environments where censorship is prevalent. Web3 also has the potential to empower individuals by providing new economic opportunities through decentralized applications and the creation of digital assets. Finally, by enabling users to control their online identity and assets, Web3 offers a more democratic and equitable internet, where users have more agency and control over their online experience. Overall, the impact of Web3 is far-reaching, and its potential to transform the internet and society is immense.

THE PROBLEMS WITH THE CURRENT INTERNET
The Problems with the Current Internet

The internet has transformed how we communicate, access information, and do business. However, despite its many benefits, the current internet is facing several challenges that limit its potential and hinder its growth. One of the most pressing problems is centralization, which gives a few large companies control most of the internet's content and data. This centralization has led to several privacy and security issues, censorship, and restriction of access to information.

Centralization of the Internet

The internet is dominated by a few large companies that control most of its content and data. These companies have become gatekeepers of the internet, with the power to control what information is available, who has access to it, and how it is used. This centralization has created several problems, including:

Censorship: The centralization of the internet has given these companies the power to censor and restrict access to information. This censorship can take many forms, from blocking access to websites to filtering search results. The censorship of information can also have a significant impact on free speech and the exchange of ideas.

Privacy Concerns: The centralization of the internet has also created significant privacy concerns. Large companies collect vast amounts of personal data and use it for various purposes, including targeted advertising, market research, and data analysis. This data can also be sold to other companies. In some cases, it can be used to influence political decisions.

Security Risks: Centralized systems are vulnerable to security breaches, as they are controlled by a single point of failure. Hackers and cybercriminals can target these central points and steal sensitive information, causing significant damage to individuals, businesses, and society as a whole.

The Privacy Issues Facing the Current Internet

The internet also poses significant privacy risks to individuals, businesses, and society. These risks are mainly due to large companies' collection and use of personal data and the vulnerability of centralized systems to cyberattacks. Some of the key privacy issues facing the current internet include:

Data Collection: Large companies collect vast amounts of personal data from users, including their browsing history, search queries, and location data. This data is used for various purposes, including targeted advertising, market research, and data analysis.

Data Breaches: Centralized systems are vulnerable to data breaches, which can result in the theft of sensitive personal information. This information can be used for malicious purposes, such as identity theft or financial fraud.

Data Monetization: Companies monetize the personal data they collect by selling it to other companies, who use it for various purposes. This can include targeted advertising, market research, and data analysis.

Conclusion

The current internet is facing significant challenges due to centralization and privacy issues. These problems limit the potential of the internet and hinder its growth. They also pose significant risks to individuals, businesses, and society. The next generation of the internet, known as Web3, represents a shift from a centralized to a decentralized architecture, and it has the potential to provide solutions to many of the most pressing problems facing the current internet. By putting users in control of their online presence and data, Web3 offers a more secure and trustworthy platform for communication, commerce, and information sharing.

DECENTRALIZATION
Decentralization

The internet has changed the world in many ways. Still, it has created several problems, including centralization, privacy concerns, and security risks. A new generation of the internet, known as Web3, has emerged to address these problems. Unlike the current internet, dominated by a few large companies, Web3 is based on a decentralized architecture that lets users control their online presence and data.

What is Decentralization?

Decentralization refers to a system in which power and decision-making authority are distributed among multiple actors rather than concentrated in a single central authority. For example, on the internet, decentralization means that users control their online identity and data and can interact with the internet securely and trustfully.

The Decentralized Architecture of Web3

Web3 is built on a decentralized architecture that is designed to address the problems of the current internet. At the heart of Web3 is a network of decentralized nodes connected to each other through a secure, peer-to-peer (P2P) protocol. This network enables users to interact with the internet and with each other securely and trust-based without relying on centralized intermediaries.

The Benefits of Decentralization

The decentralized architecture of Web3 offers several key benefits, including:

Security: Decentralization reduces the risk of security breaches by eliminating single points of failure. With no central authority controlling the network, hackers and cybercriminals cannot target a single point to steal sensitive information.

Privacy: Web3 enables users to control their online identity and data and to interact with the internet in a secure and privacy-friendly way. With no central authority collecting and monetizing personal data, users can keep their information safe from third-party companies and cyber criminals.

Trust: The decentralized architecture of Web3 enables users to interact with the internet and with each other in a trust-based way. By eliminating the need for intermediaries, Web3 offers a more secure and trustworthy platform for communication, commerce, and information sharing.

Censorship Resistance: Web3 is designed to be censorship-resistant, providing a platform for free expression and the exchange of ideas, even in environments where censorship is prevalent.

Economic Empowerment: Web3 provides new economic opportunities through decentralized applications and the creation of digital assets. By enabling users to control their online identity and assets, Web3 offers a more democratic and equitable internet, where users have more agency and control over their online experience.

The Disadvantages of Decentralization

Decentralization has several disadvantages, including:

Lack of scalability: Decentralized systems can often be slow and inefficient due to the sheer number of nodes involved in the network. This can result in a lack of scalability and make it difficult for decentralized systems to handle large amounts of data and transactions.

* * *

Lack of security: Decentralized systems can be vulnerable to attacks, as they need a central authority to regulate and secure the network. This can result in security breaches and the loss of sensitive information.

Complexity: Decentralized systems can be complex to understand and use, especially for individuals who are not familiar with the technology. This can result in a lack of adoption and limit decentralized systems' growth and potential.

Lack of standardization: Decentralized systems can often be fragmented and lack standardization, which can result in compatibility issues between different decentralized systems. This can limit the ability of decentralized systems to interoperate and exchange information.

Lack of incentives: Decentralized systems often rely on community-driven participation and contribution, which can be difficult to incentivize and maintain. This can result in a lack of individual participation and engagement, which can limit the growth and potential of decentralized systems.

Conclusion

Web3 is a new generation of the internet that is based on a decentralized architecture. This architecture offers several key benefits, including security, privacy, trust, censorship resistance, and economic empowerment. By putting users in control of their online presence and data, Web3 offers a more secure and trustworthy platform for communication, commerce, and information sharing. The decentralized architecture of Web3 represents a shift from the centralized, intermediated model of the current internet, and it has the potential to revolutionize how we interact with the internet and each other.

PRIVACY IN WEB3
Privacy in web3

The internet has become an integral part of our daily lives. Still, it has also created new privacy concerns and security risks. With the rise of big data and the increasing use of personal data by companies and governments, the need for a more secure and privacy-friendly internet has become more pressing. A new generation of the internet, known as Web3, has emerged to address these problems. Unlike the current internet, dominated by a few large companies, Web3 is based on a decentralized architecture that lets users control their online presence and data.

The Problems with Privacy on the Current Internet

The internet is dominated by centralized intermediaries, such as social media platforms, search engines, and e-commerce sites. These intermediaries collect, store, and monetize personal data, which can be used to target users with personalized advertisements, to sell to data brokers, or to be shared with governments.

In addition to privacy concerns, the internet also suffers from security risks, such as data breaches, hacking, and identity theft. With centralized intermediaries storing sensitive information, users must trust these companies to keep their data safe. However, this trust is often misplaced, as companies have been repeatedly shown to be vulnerable to security breaches and hacking attacks.

The Privacy Benefits of Web3

Web3 is designed to address the privacy and security problems of the current internet. By eliminating the need for intermediaries, Web3 offers a more secure and privacy-friendly platform for communication, commerce, and information sharing. Some of the critical privacy benefits of Web3 include the following:

Data Ownership: Web3 enables users to own and control their personal data rather than having it collected and monetized by centralized intermediaries. With users in control of their data, they can decide who has access to it and how it is used.

Privacy-Preserving Technologies: Web3 is built on privacy-preserving technologies that protect users' personal information and online activity, such as encryption and anonymization.

Decentralized Identity: Web3 provides users with a decentralized identity that they can use to securely and privately interact with the internet and each other. This eliminates the need for users to share personal information with centralized intermediaries and reduces the risk of identity theft.

Security: Decentralization reduces the risk of security breaches by eliminating single points of failure. With no central authority controlling the network, hackers and cybercriminals cannot target a single point to steal sensitive information.

The Future of Privacy with Web3

Web3 represents a shift from the centralized, intermediated model of the current internet to a decentralized, user-controlled platform. With users controlling their online identity and data, Web3 offers a more secure and privacy-friendly platform for communication, commerce, and information sharing. As Web3 continues to evolve, it has the potential to revolutionize the way we think about privacy and security on the internet.

Conclusion

The need for a more secure and privacy-friendly internet has never been greater, and Web3 is well-positioned to meet that need. With its decentralized architecture and privacy-preserving technologies, Web3 offers users a more secure and private platform for communication, commerce, and information sharing. By putting users in control of their online identity and data, Web3 represents a significant step forward in the evolution of the internet and in protecting personal privacy and security.

CENSORSHIP RESISTANCE
Censorship Resistance

In today's world, censorship is a growing concern for many individuals and organizations who rely on the internet to communicate, share information, and express their opinions. The internet, dominated by a few large companies and centralized intermediaries, has made it easier for governments and other powerful actors to monitor and restrict online content. This censorship can range from blocking access to websites and services, filtering or manipulating search results, and punishing those who express dissent.

The Problems with Censorship on the Current Internet

The current internet is not designed to protect against censorship. With centralized intermediaries controlling access to information and communication, they can be easily targeted by governments and other actors to restrict or remove content. This can have a chilling effect on free speech and limit access to information for users.

In addition to censorship, the current internet also faces problems of information manipulation, such as fake news and propaganda, which can be spread through social media and other online channels. This manipulation can significantly impact public opinion and the democratic process.

The Censorship Resistance of Web3

Web3 offers a censorship-resistant platform for information sharing using a decentralized architecture that eliminates the need for intermediaries. This decentralized structure provides several benefits for censorship resistance, including:

Decentralized Infrastructure: With no central control point, Web3 is much harder to censor than the current internet. Governments and other actors cannot target a single point to restrict access to information and communication.

Encryption and Anonymization: Web3 is built on privacy-preserving technologies that protect users' personal information and online activity, such as encryption and anonymization. This makes it harder for governments and other actors to monitor and restrict content.

Decentralized Identity: Web3 provides users with a decentralized identity that they can use to securely and privately interact with the internet and each other. This eliminates the need for users to share personal information with centralized intermediaries, reducing the risk of censorship.

Decentralized Applications: Web3 is powered by decentralized applications (dapps) that are not controlled by any single entity. Governments or other actors must keep them from being shut down or censored.

The Future of Censorship Resistance with Web3

Web3 represents a significant step forward in the fight against censorship. By eliminating the need for intermediaries and providing a decentralized platform for information sharing, Web3 makes it much harder for governments and other actors to restrict or manipulate online content. Moreover, as Web3 continues to evolve, it has the potential to provide a more open and accessible platform for communication and information sharing, enabling users to express their opinions and access information without fear of censorship.

Conclusion

The internet has become essential for communication, sharing information, and free expression. Still, it has also become a tool for censorship and information manipulation. Web3 offers a solution to these problems by providing a censorship-resistant platform for information sharing, built on a decentralized architecture that eliminates the need for intermediaries. By putting users in control of their online identity and data, Web3 represents a significant step forward in the fight against censorship and protecting free expression and access to information.

TRUST AND SECURITY
Trust and Security

In the current internet, trust is often established through intermediaries, such as banks, payment processors, and centralized servers. These intermediaries act as trusted third parties, verifying transactions and safeguarding personal information. However, this reliance on intermediaries also creates potential vulnerabilities and points of failure. For example, intermediaries can be hacked, go out of business, or misuse customer data, leading to financial losses and privacy violations.

The Problems with Intermediaries on the Current Internet

The internet is built on a centralized architecture that requires intermediaries to establish trust and secure transactions. As a result, this system is vulnerable to several types of attacks, including:

Hacks: Intermediaries, with access to large amounts of sensitive personal and financial information, are targets for hackers and cybercriminals. These attacks can lead to data breaches and financial losses.

Misuse of Customer Data: Intermediaries often collect and store vast amounts of personal information, which can be misused or sold to third parties without consent.

Single Point of Failure: With all transactions and data passing through a single intermediary, a breach or failure at this single point can have serious consequences for customers.

The Trust and Security of Web3

Web3 eliminates the need for intermediaries by using decentralized technology to establish trust and secure transactions. This decentralized architecture provides several benefits for trust and security, including:

Decentralized Ledgers: Web3 is built on decentralized ledgers distributed across many nodes, such as the blockchain. This eliminates the need for intermediaries and provides a secure and transparent transaction platform.

Encryption and Anonymization: Web3 uses privacy-preserving technologies, such as encryption and anonymization, to protect users' personal information and transactions.

Decentralized Identity: Web3 provides users with a decentralized identity that they can use to securely and privately interact with the internet and each other. This eliminates the need for users to share personal information with intermediaries, reducing the risk of data breaches and misuse.

Decentralized Applications: Web3 is powered by decentralized applications (dapps) that are not controlled by any single entity. This eliminates the risk of a single failure point and gives users more control over their data and transactions.

The Future of Trust and Security with Web3

Web3 represents a significant step forward in trust and security by eliminating the need for intermediaries and providing a decentralized platform for transactions. With the ability to secure transactions and personal information through decentralized ledgers, encryption, and decentralized identity, Web3 provides a more secure platform for transactions and online interactions. As Web3 continues to evolve, it has the potential to provide a more trustworthy and secure internet, reducing the risks of data breaches and financial losses.

Conclusion

The current internet relies on intermediaries to establish trust and secure transactions. Still, this system is vulnerable to data breaches, financial losses, and privacy violations. Web3 eliminates the need for intermediaries by using decentralized technology to establish trust and secure transactions. This decentralized architecture gives users more control over their data and transactions. It reduces the risks of data breaches and financial losses. By providing a more secure platform for transactions, Web3 represents a significant step forward in trust and security for the internet.

ECONOMIC EMPOWERMENT
Economic Empowerment

The current internet has enabled the creation and exchange of vast information. Still, it has yet to be as successful in enabling the creation and exchange of value. The existing economic model is dominated by centralized intermediaries, such as banks, payment processors, and online marketplaces, which control access to capital and extract fees and rent from users. This centralized economic model has created economic disparities and left many needing access to capital and financial services.

The Problems with the Current Economic Model on the Internet

The current economic model on the internet is characterized by several problems, including:

Financial Inclusion: The current financial system is designed to exclude many people from accessing capital and financial services. Over 1.7 billion people are unbanked and need access to traditional financial services, making it difficult for them to participate in the global economy.

Rent-Seeking Intermediaries: Intermediaries extract fees and rent from users, reducing the value created and exchanged. This rent-seeking behavior creates inefficiencies and reduces the overall economic impact of the internet.

Lack of Ownership and Control: Users need ownership and control over their data and assets, which are controlled by centralized intermediaries. This limits users' ability to monetize their data and assets and reduces the overall economic impact of the internet.

The Economic Empowerment of Web3

Web3 provides a new decentralized economic model for creating and exchanging value, eliminating the need for intermediaries and enabling users to participate in the global economy. This decentralized economic model provides several benefits for economic empowerment, including:

Financial Inclusion: Web3 provides a platform for financial inclusion, enabling unbanked people to access capital and financial services. This opens up new economic opportunities and enables people to participate globally.

Decentralized Finance (DeFi): Web3 provides a platform for decentralized finance (DeFi), a new financial system built on decentralized technology. DeFi enables users to access financial services, such as lending, borrowing, and investing, without intermediaries.

Tokenization: Web3 enables the tokenization of assets, which is the process of representing ownership of an asset as a digital token. Tokenization enables users to monetize their assets and data, creating new economic opportunities.

Decentralized Applications (dapps): Web3 provides a platform for decentralized applications (dapps), which are not controlled by any single entity. dapps enable users to create and exchange value in a decentralized and trustless manner, reducing the need for intermediaries and increasing economic efficiency.

The Future of Economic Empowerment with Web3

Web3 represents a significant step forward in economic empowerment by providing a new decentralized economic model for creating and exchanging value. By enabling financial inclusion, decentralized finance, tokenization, and decentralized applications, Web3 provides a platform for people to participate in the global economy and monetize their assets and data. As Web3 continues to evolve, it has the potential to provide a more inclusive and equitable economic model, reducing economic disparities and empowering people to create and exchange value on a global scale.

Conclusion

The current economic model on the internet is dominated by centralized intermediaries, which control access to capital and extract fees and rent from users. Web3 provides a new decentralized economic model for creating and exchanging value, eliminating the need for intermediaries and enabling users to participate in the global economy. In addition, this decentralized economic model provides financial inclusion.

DECENTRALIZED APPLICATIONS
Decentralized Applications

The internet has enabled the creation and exchange of vast amounts of information. Still, it has yet to be as successful in enabling the creation and exchange of value. The existing economic model is dominated by centralized intermediaries, such as banks, payment processors, and online marketplaces, which control access to capital and extract fees and rent from users. Web3 provides a new decentralized economic model for creating and exchanging value, eliminating the need for intermediaries and enabling users to participate in the global economy.

One of the critical components of the Web3 ecosystem is decentralized applications, or dapps, which are applications built on a decentralized platform. dapps have the potential to disrupt various industries and provide new economic opportunities by enabling users to create and exchange value in a decentralized and trustless manner.

What are Decentralized Applications (dapps)?

A decentralized application (dapp) is an application built on a decentralized platform, such as the Ethereum blockchain, which operates on a decentralized network of nodes. dapps are not controlled by any single entity and are instead governed by a set of rules encoded in smart contracts. This enables dapps to operate in a trustless and transparent manner without the need for intermediaries.

The Benefits of Decentralized Applications (dapps)

dapps provide several benefits over traditional centralized applications, including:

Decentralization: dapps are decentralized and not controlled by any single entity, giving users more control over their data and assets.

Security: dapps operate on a decentralized network of nodes, making them less vulnerable to hacking and security breaches.

Trustlessness: dapps operate on a trustless platform, eliminating the need for intermediaries and reducing the risk of fraud and corruption.

Transparency: dapps operate on a transparent platform, providing users with a clear view of how their data and assets are used.

The Challenges of Decentralized Applications (dapps)

Decentralized applications (dapps) have several disadvantages, including:

Complexity: dapps can be complex to use and understand, especially for individuals who are not familiar with the technology. This can result in a lack of adoption and limit the growth and potential of dapps.

Scalability: dapps can often suffer from scalability issues, as they are built on decentralized networks that can become congested and slow. This can make it difficult for dapps to handle large amounts of data and transactions, limiting their potential.

Security: dapps can be vulnerable to security threats as they do not have a central authority to regulate and secure the network. This can result in security breaches and the loss of sensitive information.

Lack of Regulation: dapps are often built on decentralized networks outside traditional regulatory frameworks. This can result in a lack of accountability and make it difficult for individuals to resolve disputes or seek compensation in the case of a problem. This lack of regulation can make it difficult for dapps to gain widespread adoption and legitimacy.

Potential Impact of Decentralized Applications (dapps) on Various Industries

dapps have the potential to disrupt various industries and provide new economic opportunities. Some of the industries that are likely to be impacted by dapps include:

Financial Services: dapps can disrupt the financial services industry by enabling users to access financial services, such as lending, borrowing, and investing, without intermediaries. This reduces the cost of financial services and gives users more control over their assets and data. For example, decentralized finance (DeFi) apps allow users to participate in the global financial market without needing a traditional bank or financial institution. DeFi platforms such as Aave and Uniswap enable users to lend, borrow, and trade assets in a decentralized and trustless manner.

Gaming: dapps can disrupt the gaming industry by enabling users to own and trade in-game assets in a decentralized and trustless manner. This creates new economic opportunities for game developers and users. For example, the blockchain-based game CryptoKitties enables users to breed and trade digital cats. At the same time, Decentraland is a virtual reality platform where users can buy and sell virtual land, build and monetize virtual content, and engage in virtual commerce.

E-commerce: dapps have the potential to disrupt the e-commerce industry by enabling users to buy and sell goods and services in a decentralized and trustless manner. This reduces the cost of e-commerce and provides users with more control over their data and assets. For example, the decentralized marketplace OpenBazaar enables users.

Conclusion

In conclusion, decentralized applications built on Web3 have the potential to revolutionize various industries and change the way we interact with technology. With their decentralized architecture, dapps eliminate the need for intermediaries, provide greater privacy and security, and offer a new, more democratic model for creating and exchanging value. However, the impact of these apps still needs to be discovered. Still, as more developers and users adopt Web3 technology, we expect to see a new wave of innovation that will challenge the status quo and bring a more decentralized, equitable, and secure internet.

THE FUTURE OF WEB3

The Future of Web3

The future of Web3 is promising, and several trends and technologies will shape its trajectory in the coming years.

Let's take a look at the topics that will dominate web3

Decentralized finance (DeFi)

The growth of DeFi has been phenomenal in recent years, and it is likely to continue to grow as more people seek to take advantage of its benefits. DeFi allows financial services to be provided on a decentralized and trustless platform, eliminating the need for intermediaries and reducing the risk of censorship or interference.

Non-Fungible Tokens (NFTs)

NFTs are unique digital assets stored on a blockchain. They have gained popularity in recent years, especially in the art world. The future of NFTs looks bright. They will likely become more widely adopted in the coming years as more people seek to monetize their digital creations and digital assets.

Decentralized Autonomous Organizations (DAOs)

DAOs are organizations that are run by a set of rules encoded as smart contracts on a blockchain, and they are designed to be decentralized, transparent, and secure. The future of DAOs looks bright, and they will likely become more widely adopted as more people seek to build decentralized organizations resistant to censorship and interference.

Interoperability

Interoperability refers to the ability of different blockchain platforms to work together seamlessly. Interoperability is essential for the future of Web3, as it will allow different blockchain platforms to communicate and exchange information, leading to greater efficiency, scalability, and innovation.

Scalability

Scalability is a significant challenge for Web3, and it refers to the ability of a blockchain platform to handle a large number of transactions and users without becoming slow or congested. Scalability is essential for the future of Web3, as it will determine the platform's ability to support real-world applications and reach mass adoption.

Privacy

Privacy is a significant concern for many people. Privacy-focused solutions will likely become more popular as people seek to protect their data and digital assets. Web3 platforms will need to provide robust privacy solutions that are easy to use and allow users to control their data and digital assets.

Conclusion

In conclusion, the future of Web3 is bright and full of potential, and several trends and technologies will shape its trajectory in the coming years. Decentralized finance, non-fungible tokens, decentralized autonomous organizations, interoperability, scalability, and privacy are some key trends and technologies that will shape the future of Web3. As Web3 continues to evolve, it will create a more open, transparent, and equitable online ecosystem where users will have greater control and ownership over their data and digital assets.

INVESTMENT OPPORTUNITIES
Investment Opportunities

Investment opportunities in Web3 and its underlying technology are attracting attention from a wide range of investors, from individuals to institutional investors. The potential for growth and innovation in the Web3 space is immense and has created a new asset class: Web3 investments. In this chapter, we will analyze the investment opportunities in Web3 and its underlying technology.

Web3 Investment Themes

The Web3 space is rapidly evolving, and there are several key investment themes that investors should be aware of. These themes include:

Decentralized Finance (DeFi)

Decentralized finance is a new financial system built on blockchain technology that allows individuals to participate in financial markets without intermediaries. DeFi has attracted significant investment and is one of the most promising areas for growth in the Web3 space.

Decentralized Identity

Decentralized identity is a new way of managing personal information and data that eliminates the need for intermediaries. This can change how individuals interact with the internet and is attracting significant investment.

Decentralized Social Media

Decentralized social media is a new way of interacting with others online that eliminates the need for intermediaries. This theme can change how individuals interact with each other online and is attracting significant investment.

Decentralized Marketplaces

Decentralized marketplaces are a new way of buying and selling goods and services that eliminates the need for intermediaries. This theme can change how individuals interact with the internet and is attracting significant investment.

Investment Vehicles

Several investment vehicles are available for individuals interested in investing in Web3 and its underlying technology. These vehicles include:

Cryptocurrency Exchanges

Cryptocurrency exchanges allow individuals to buy and sell cryptocurrencies. They are one of the most popular investment vehicles for Web3 investments.

Decentralized Exchanges (DEXs)

Decentralized exchanges allow individuals to buy and sell cryptocurrencies without intermediaries. They are becoming increasingly popular as a means of investing in Web3 and its underlying technology.

Initial Coin Offerings (ICOs)

Initial coin offerings are a way for companies to raise capital by issuing new cryptocurrencies. They are becoming increasingly popular as a means of investing in Web3 and its underlying technology.

Risks and Considerations

Investing in Web3 and its underlying technology is not without risk. There are several key risks and considerations that investors should be aware of, including:

Regulatory Risk

The regulatory environment for Web3 and its underlying technology is uncertain and subject to change. This creates regulatory risk for investors.

Liquidity Risk

The liquidity of Web3 investments is uncertain and is subject to change. This creates liquidity risk for investors.

Technological Risk

The underlying technology of Web3 is rapidly evolving and is subject to change. This creates technological risk for investors.

How to start investing in web3?

Investing in Web3 can be a promising opportunity. Still, it can also be a complex and challenging process for those new to the technology. Here are some steps that you can follow to start investing in Web3:

Research: Before investing in any asset, it's essential to conduct thorough research and understand the basics of the technology. In the case of Web3, you should familiarize yourself with decentralized networks, blockchain technology, and various Web3 assets, such as decentralized applications (dapps) and Web3 tokens.

***

Determine your investment goals: It's essential to determine your goals before making any investments. For example, are you looking to hold your investment for the long term, or are you looking for short-term gain? This will help you determine which assets best suit your investment strategy.

Choose a reliable exchange: To invest in Web3 assets, you must choose a reliable exchange that allows you to buy, sell, and trade these assets. Look for an exchange that has a good reputation, is regulated, and provides adequate security measures to protect your assets. A good starting point would OpenSea or Coinbase.

Choose your assets: After selecting an exchange, you can choose the Web3 assets you want to invest in. This can include dapps, Web3 tokens, and other decentralized assets. It's essential to consider factors such as the asset's growth potential, adoption rate, and community support before deciding.

* * *

Diversify your portfolio: Diversification is critical when investing in any asset class, and Web3 is no exception. Consider investing in a mix of different Web3 assets to reduce risk and increase your chances of success.

Keep an eye on the market: Like any asset class, the value of Web3 assets can be impacted by market conditions and other external factors. Therefore, keeping an eye on the market and staying informed about the latest developments in the Web3 space is essential.

Seek professional advice: If you are new to investing or feel uncertain about the process, consider seeking professional advice from a financial advisor or a knowledgeable person in the Web3 space.

Investing in Web3 can be a promising opportunity. Still, it's crucial to approach it cautiously and consider all the factors involved. By conducting thorough research, determining your investment goals, choosing a reliable exchange, and seeking professional advice, you can increase your chances of success when investing in Web3.

Conclusion

In conclusion, investment opportunities in Web3 and its underlying technology are attracting attention from a wide range of investors. The potential for growth and innovation in the Web3 space is immense and has created a new asset class: Web3 investments. Several investment vehicles are available for individuals interested in investing in Web3 and its underlying technology, including cryptocurrency exchanges, decentralized exchanges, initial coin offerings, and venture capital funds.

TECHNICAL ASPECTS OF WEB3
Technical Aspects of web3

Unlike the traditional web, centralized and controlled by a few powerful entities, Web3 is built on a decentralized network of nodes that allows for a more open, transparent, and secure internet. In this chapter, we will explore the technical aspects of Web3 and how they contribute to its potential as a new internet infrastructure.

The underlying technology of Web3: Blockchain

Web3 is built on blockchain technology, a decentralized ledger that records transactions securely and transparently. In a blockchain, transactions are verified and processed by a network of nodes rather than a central authority. This creates a tamper-proof record of transactions that is publicly accessible and can be audited by anyone.

One of the most popular blockchain technologies used in Web3 is the Ethereum blockchain. Ethereum is a decentralized platform that allows developers to build and deploy decentralized applications (dapps) on its network. Ethereum also has its own cryptocurrency, Ether (ETH), which is used as a form of payment for transaction fees and computational services on the network.

Decentralized applications (dapps)

Decentralized applications (dapps) are the backbone of the Web3 infrastructure. They are applications that run on a decentralized network, eliminating the need for a central authority to control and regulate the application. This results in a more open, transparent, and secure application resistant to censorship and data breaches.

Dapps are typically built on blockchain technology, ranging from simple applications like decentralized marketplaces to complex applications like decentralized autonomous organizations (DAOs). Some famous examples of dapps in the Web3 space include Uniswap, a decentralized exchange for trading cryptocurrencies, and Compound, a decentralized lending and borrowing platform.

Web3 tokens

Web3 tokens are digital assets that can be used as a form of payment or to represent ownership within a dapp. They are typically built on blockchain technology, issued, and traded on decentralized exchanges. Some famous examples of Web3 tokens include Ether (ETH), which is the native cryptocurrency of the Ethereum blockchain, and DeFi tokens, which are used to represent ownership in decentralized finance (DeFi) applications.

Web3 tokens have several advantages over traditional cryptocurrencies, such as Bitcoin. For example, Web3 tokens are more flexible and represent a broader range of assets, such as real estate or stocks. They are also more interoperable, allowing them to be easily traded and used within different dapps on the Web3 network.

Web3 Identity

Web3 identity is a crucial aspect of the Web3 infrastructure that aims to provide individuals with control over their personal data and privacy. In the traditional web, personal data is often stored by centralized entities and can be easily accessed and used for targeted advertising and other purposes.

In contrast, Web3 identity allows individuals to own and control their personal data, which can be stored on a decentralized network and accessed with their permission. This results in a more secure and private internet where individuals can control their personal data and choose who has access to it.

Web3 identity is typically implemented through decentralized identity (DID) protocols, which allow individuals to create and manage their own digital identity on the blockchain. This results in a more secure and private internet where individuals can control their personal data and choose who has access to it.

Conclusion

Web3 is a new, exciting internet infrastructure offering a more open, secure, and transparent internet for individuals and businesses. Its technical aspects, including blockchain technology, decentralized applications, Web 3 tokens, and Web3 identity, contribute to its potential as a new and improved internet infrastructure. The decentralized nature of Web3 allows for greater privacy, security, and freedom for individuals and businesses, and its flexible and interoperable design enables a wide range of applications and uses cases.

However, the Web3 infrastructure is still in its early stages of development, and some challenges, such as scalability and user adoption, need to be addressed. Nevertheless, the potential of Web3 is immense, and it has the potential to transform the way we interact with the internet and each other.

As Web3 continues to evolve and mature, it will be interesting to see how it develops and impacts various industries and the world. It is a promising future, and the technical aspects of Web3 will play a critical role in determining its success.

WEB3 PITFALLS AND RISKS
web3 Pitfalls and Risks

Web3, also known as the decentralized web, is a new paradigm for the internet that aims to provide a secure, transparent, and equitable platform for exchanging value and information. While Web3 has the potential to revolutionize the internet and provide a range of benefits over the current centralized systems, it has its risks and challenges.

This chapter aims to provide a comprehensive overview of the potential pitfalls and risks associated with Web3, including security concerns, scalability issues, and regulatory challenges. It will also cover potential drawbacks of decentralized systems, such as the difficulties in reversing transactions and the lack of centralized control.

Security Concerns

One of the most significant risks associated with Web3 is security. As Web3 relies on decentralized networks, it is susceptible to malicious actors who may seek to exploit vulnerabilities in the system. For example, hackers could target smart contracts, the code that powers decentralized applications, and steal funds or manipulate transactions.

Additionally, there is a risk of 51% attacks, where a single entity or group of entities control over half of the network's computational power. This allows them to manipulate the network, double-spend coins, and interfere with the validation of transactions.

Scalability Issues

Another challenge facing Web3 is scalability. Decentralized systems are inherently slower and less efficient than centralized systems due to their reliance on many nodes to validate transactions. This can result in slow transaction processing times and high fees, making it difficult for Web3 to handle many transactions.

To address scalability issues, Web3 networks are continually exploring and implementing new technologies, such as sharding and off-chain transactions, to increase efficiency and reduce the number of nodes required to validate transactions.

Regulatory Challenges

Web3 is still a relatively new and untested technology subject to regulatory uncertainty. Governments and regulatory bodies may seek to impose restrictions on Web3 and its underlying technology, including cryptocurrencies, to prevent money laundering and other illicit activities.

Furthermore, the decentralized nature of Web3 means that it is difficult to regulate, making it a potential target for regulators looking to control and monitor online transactions.

Lack of Centralized Control

One of the benefits of Web3 is its decentralized architecture, which eliminates the need for intermediaries and provides a more secure platform for transactions. However, this lack of centralized control can also be a drawback in certain circumstances.

For example, suppose a user loses access to their private key, the cryptographic key that grants access to their Web3 assets. In that case, there needs to be a centralized authority to assist them in recovering their funds. Additionally, in the event of a bug or vulnerability in the code of a decentralized application, there may not be a centralized entity to patch the issue, leaving users at risk.

Conclusion

In conclusion, while Web3 has the potential to revolutionize the internet and provide a range of benefits over the current centralized systems, it has its risks and challenges. Security, scalability, regulatory challenges, and the lack of centralized control are all potential drawbacks that need to be considered by anyone looking to participate in the Web3 ecosystem.

It is essential to thoroughly research and understand the technology and the projects invested in and familiarize oneself with the associated risks. By doing so, individuals can make informed decisions and minimize the potential risks associated with Web3.

CONCLUSION
Conclusion

The chapters above provide an overview of Web3. This decentralized technology aims to address the centralization and privacy issues of the current internet. These chapters cover various topics, including the basics of decentralized technology, the benefits of decentralization, user privacy protection, censorship resistance, trust and security, economic empowerment, decentralized applications, the future of Web3, investment opportunities, and the technical aspects of Web3. Additionally, there is a chapter on the potential pitfalls and risks of decentralized technology, including the challenges and drawbacks of Web3. These chapters provide a comprehensive overview of Web3 and its underlying technology. They are aimed at beginners looking to understand the basics of this exciting and rapidly evolving field.

I hope you enjoyed reading this book. If you did, I would appreciate a review on Amazon. Also, if you have any feedback, please email me at ralph@kuepper.io.

www.ingramcontent.com/pod-product-compliance
Lightning Source LLC
Chambersburg PA
CBHW070321220526
45465CB00013B/2048